W9-DFC-270

Mrs. Dumpty

The Felix Pollak Prize in Poetry
The University of Wisconsin Press Poetry Series
Ronald Wallace, General Editor

Now We're Getting Somewhere • David Clewell
Henry Taylor, Judge, 1994

The Legend of Light • Bob Hicok
Carolyn Kizer, Judge, 1995

Fragments in Us: Recent and Earlier Poems • Dennis Trudell
Philip Levine, Judge, 1996

Don't Explain • Betsy Sholl
Rita Dove, Judge, 1997

Mrs. Dumpty • Chana Bloch
Donald Hall, Judge, 1998

Mrs. Dumpty

Chana Bloch

The University of Wisconsin Press

The University of Wisconsin Press
2537 Daniels Street
Madison, Wisconsin 53718

3 Henrietta Street
London WC2E 8LU, England

Library of Congress Cataloging-in-Publication Data
Bloch, Chana.
Mrs. Dumpty / Chana Bloch.
80 pp.   cm. (Felix Pollak prize in poetry)
ISBN 0-299-16000-9 (cloth: alk. paper).
ISBN 0-299-16004-1 (pbk.: alk. paper)
I. Title.   II. Series: Felix Pollak prize in poetry (Series)
PS3552.L548 M77   1998
811'.54 ddc21   98-26433

Any real change implies the breakup of the world
as one has always known it, the loss of all that
gave one an identity, the end of safety.

—James Baldwin

Contents

Acknowledgments

My thanks to the editors of the following journals, where these poems
first appeared (some in earlier versions or with different titles):

The Atlantic Monthly: "Tired Sex"

Field: "Self-Portrait at 11:30 P.M.," "The Conservation of Energy"

The Marlboro Review: "Mother Hunger"(winner of the Marlboro Prize)

The Nation: "Trompe l'Oeil"

The New Yorker: "Mrs. Dumpty"

Ploughshares: "The Collector"

Poetry: "Visiting Hours are Over," "Though You Haven't Asked"

Salmagundi: "The Archipelago of Dreams," "The Equilibrists," "In the
Ward"

The Threepenny Review: "What It Takes"

The Virginia Quarterly Review: "The Comforters," "Rehearsal," "How
the Last Act Begins"

"Tired Sex" and "Clear and Cold" were set to music by David Del
Tredici as part of the song cycle, "Chana's Story."

Finally, profound gratitude to my children, for their strength and wis-
dom. To my dear family of friends, for sustenance. To my poetry
buddies, for their demanding criticism. And to Yaddo, where many
of these poems were written in four restorative summers.

Mrs. Dumpty

The last time the doctors gave up
I put the pieces together
and bought him a blue wool jacket, a shirt
and a tie with scribbles of magenta,
brown buckle shoes. I dressed him
and sat him down
with a hankie in his pocket folded into points.
Then a shell knit slowly
over his sad starched heart.

He'd laugh and dangle his long legs and call out,
What a fall that was!
And I'd sing the refrain,
What a fall!

And now he's at my door again, begging
in that leaky voice,
and I start wiping the smear
from his broken face.

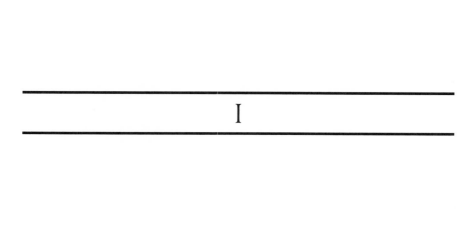

I

Hosanna

For the way we met between floors on the staircase
(He's the one, said Martha),
for the salt of your cheek and the silky
crook of your elbow,
the secondhand mattress with its geography of stains,
for the spirits of Berkeley whose names
I didn't know yet
(jasmine, said Sharon, *azalea, camellia, rhododendron,*
and I scribbled it all down like a student),
for the sticky
imprint of your sweat up and down my body
as we studied each other,
for your honeymoon kisses at dawn
and Dubrovnik still green *(Have a Good Trip with*
ENA Motoring Oil, the billboard blessing
in Serbo-Croatian),
for the thermos that broke when I opened the car door
(It's good luck, we warned each other),
the old woman in the park who offered us dark bread and cheese
with a cackle of *Bitte, bitte,*
the one word of Foreign she knew,
for the red fox that startled us, the two trees that rose
from a single charred trunk,
the monks chanting plainsong in the church near Zagreb
that burned down in the war
(Hosanna, they sang),
for each loss that sparks another like kisses
we stay up all night for
wherever they lead.

Please Hold

You used to imitate a camel
eating—nostrils flared, your dogged
hilarious jaw
sawing left and right. It was easy
to love you then.

I'd start coq au vin
on the pokey two-burner,
James Beard propped open with a pot.

That time we dialed Pan Am and danced
to their "Please Hold" fox trot, Mulligan's
honey-slow horn, remember?
the telephone pressed between us. . . .

We'd drowse off at midnight, a muddle
of arms and legs
till your cock-crow under the covers
awakened us both.

And then there was morning. I'd steal
one last-minute dream
and open my eyes to a blur
of Burma Shave
in the bathroom doorway, a fizz of sunrise

you wiped away, then
two-stepped toward me.

Act One

Hedda Gabler is lighting the lamps in a fury.
From the front row center
we see the makeup streaking her neck,
little tassels of sweat
that stain her bodice. She says *Yes* to Tesman
and it's like spitting.

We are just-married,
feeling lucky. Between the acts
we stop to admire ourselves in the lobby mirror.

But Hedda—how misery
curdles her face!
She opens the letters with a knife
and her husband stands there
shuffling, the obliging child
waiting to be loved.

Yes, she says, fluffing the pillows
on the sofa, *yes dear*, stoking
the fire. And Tesman smiles. A shudder
jolts through her body to
lodge in mine, and
                    oh yes, I can feel that
blurt of knowledge
no bride should know.

Annunciation

The future
passed through me like light
through a prism, foot-traffic
over a bridge: two children, two
free-standing sons.
I thought I was choosing.
Light spilled through the window,
indifferent. I thought you were
choosing me. The mole on
my shoulder your earlobes our
naked teeth in their lust
to outlive us
drove us together. The past flooded me
in its milky rush to become
forever. The past in its
superabundant
waste. The angel spoke
in fire and tongues, imperturbable,
leaving me
spent on the sheets, a dazed
hand on a belly.

Happy Families Are All Alike

1

Flash of truck, blaze of
steel bearing down
burn of rubber on asphalt two tons
thundering to a stop. I can smell it,
can see that trucker
stunned, head down in his hands,
St. Christopher swinging in the window

and across the street on Colusa
in front of the school door,
hands face skinny knees, every part of him
sharply visible, outlined
in yellow light—

my son. His high voice
more plaintive than blaming:
You told me to run.

2

Who told him to run? My fault
forever. A family of before
and after. *Why did you why
did I tell him?* But look,

he's going into the classroom.
He's eating the soggy triangles
of his tuna sandwich. Nothing's
happened to us! Nothing

yet. Once upon a time, we'll say
at the family campfire,
we came *that* close.

Self-Portrait at Eleven Thirty P.M.

This is the face I serve nightly
with lace bubbles of almond soap,
head down
in the second degree of fatigue.

These are the baby breasts I buried
in my woman's bosom. Sloped shoulders.
Skinny ribcage, a fist still
beating at the bars.

Black bra, taupe stockings, long slithery
half-slip. The scar
running down my belly, ridged, opalescent.
The wild thatch they shaved off
grew back.

This is my belly, spongy, forgiving,
all its pockets picked clean.
It settles down on the stoop, drowsy:
Once I was adored.

And my feet, with their sturdy
badges of callus. All day
in the mill of my shoes
they grind, obedient.
The skin of the instep
soft as chamois.

Tired Sex

We're trying to strike a match in a matchbook
that has lain all winter under the woodpile:
damp sulphur
on sodden cardboard.
I catch myself yawning. Through the window
I watch that sparrow the cat
keeps batting around.

Like turning the pages of a book the teacher assigned—

You ought to read it, she said.
It's great literature.

Surprise Party

1

He's holding the garage door opener in his hand.
Each time he clicks,
he alters the constellations.
—He tells me this, elated:
It must be a sign.

Even the psychiatrist says it's a good dream,
but by now she's prospecting, like us,
for anything that glitters a little in the water.

2

We own a house: tan stucco, brown trim,
lamps, lamp-tables, a family
of chairs. The live oak in front
keeps us rooted.
The neighbor's cat waits for us to come home,
pads up the nineteen steps and presents
her belly to be rubbed.

And the children, of course,
our witnesses.

3

Tabbouli, black olives, Moroccan carrots,
the salads gleaming in their oils,
two days of shopping, paring and dicing,
polishing the brass. Then the toasts
and the silly candles,
the children sprawled on the floor.

Lift up your heads, O ye gates!
Linda, the world's latest widow, crowned him
Almighty King of Fifty
with a helmet of straw, his scepter
an orange studded with cloves.

He was better by then, I thought,
though he hadn't been sleeping.
I watched from the doorway, happy.

Today, still fresh from the shower,
full of a tense exuberance,
he finds me in the kitchen.
That's when it started, he wants me
to know—with Linda, there, at the party.
I don't know the welt in my throat

is anger. I take
the dishtowels from the cabinet,
fold them in two, in three,
line up their sky-blue stripes
and put them back again.

The Conservation of Energy

Why was that door locked? I want
the front door open when I get home,

and the lights on, the minute
you hear me honking. He slams

the door behind him, dashes
the porcelain bowl from the table.

Drips of oil shiver to the floor,
fork and knife, little wings

of frayed lettuce. A few
bleak words bitten off and I snap

at our son, who enters
laughing. And now

the child is pulling the cat's tail
with both hands. The cat

is storing up minus signs like a battery,
sharpening its claws.

High Summer

The sky blue-violet that evening until 10 P.M., so we drove to a lake in the park and rented a rowboat. There was an island in the middle of the lake, overgrown with willows and moss. Our older son took the oars and rowed us toward the island. The little one sat in the prow and announced: "Hey! I'll be the reporter of swan and duck news."

Sometimes a wave of happiness wells up and wipes everything clean. The water cannot contain itself. The old angers soften and sink down to the sludgy bottom. I laughed when that wave came and lifted the boat from the water.

The Comforters

1

The cat nosed around the hummingbird
but didn't want him. Sweet bird,
his throat feathers go black
then fuchsia when I tip him to the side.
Who else could I show this to but
you? I'm promoting
reasons for living. Today it's The Miracle
of Change—the rain in California, for instance,
that comes every winter to wash
the cobwebs from the leaves.
But you aren't listening.

When you give me that spooky look
I'll try anything.

2

"What are you planning for your
retirement?" sang the neighbor to my father
propped on his final
flowered pillow.
She stirred the coffee I brought her,
forked up her cake
and doled out comfort to my father the way

I talk to my husband: slowly,
as if he were a child, and too loud,
as if he were deaf or foreign, and so careful,
profusely careful, choosing
each wrong word.

Relic

That hanger I stole from the honeymoon hotel—
I've hidden it away. The kings of Europe used to kill
for a relic like that, a crumb
of the true manna, one drop of Mary's milk
in a jewelled vial.

I want you back, whoever
you used to be. I'm saving the way you'd take
the steps to our front door two at a time,
singing *Anyone home?* as your key turned
its trick in the lock.

Twenty-Fourth Anniversary

I hung my wedding dress
in the attic. I had a woolen
shoulder to lean against,
a wake-up kiss, plush words
I loved to stroke:
My husband. We.

You hung the portraits of your great-
grandparents from Stuttgart
over the sofa—boiled collar,
fashionable shawl. The yellow
shellac of marriage
coats our faces too.

We're like the neoclassical facade
on a post office. Every small town
has such a building.
Pillars forget they used to be
tree trunks, their sap congealed

into staying put. I can feel it
happening in every cell—that gradual
cooling and drying.
There is that other law of nature
which lets the dead thing stand.

17

Marcel's at 11:00

A field of snow without a track on it.

I sit myself down in the swivel chair.
Mirror, scissors, comb.
A man's hand furrowing my wet hair.

Trompe l'Oeil

The sun inflaming the horizon is really
below it already, refracted, the way
water in the pitcher bends and enlarges
the stems of the roses. A habit
of light. There's evening and then
in the morning we pull on
leftover feelings, stiff
with old sweat. *Good morning. Coffee?*
Years rise and set in the safety of
such decorum.
I feed the roses bleach from a dropper
to keep them red, stealing
a few inches of time from death—
let them stand one more day
in crystal. The violent
ghost of a sun persists. We go on
talking to each other.

Rehearsal

Driving to the airport, we pass the equestrian
statue in the park: the plumed general
on his narrow plinth. It's not easy
to sit bronzed in the traffic, splendid
in every weather. From his horse
he watches the cars plunging toward the tunnel,
three hooves stuck in cement.

I'm practicing to leave you.
Each year I leave a little more
and you drive me. Our words echo
from an undeclared distance.
Where is the ticket? I ask
though it's late to be asking.

Now I'm on the plane, buckled in, watching
a Western. That man in the blue shirt
is you, I'd pick you out anywhere.
You're taking off your boots as the wagons
tie up for the night. I knew
you'd be home by now, even with the traffic.
You're looking straight at me. So much dust
on a long journey. Dust on your cheeks,
your forehead, your hair.
I almost reach out to brush it away.

Coasting

The placid stewardess explained crash landings.
Six exits. Be careful to secure your mask.
No one listened. Now, outside the window,
ranges of unshovelled cloud.

We're coasting at thirty-two thousand
on a slope of air.
15B and C unfold skimpy blankets,
doze off like stoics in the snow.

A half-sun keeps trailing the plane. It's sunrise
or maybe sunset.
I'm wedged against the double window
with its bright beads of cold.

When the plane hits the runway
the wing slats will swing up and the brakes
clatter like kettledrums.
Whatever we've stowed overhead will go

pitching forward. I want to
stay here, tucked in among strangers
hugging toy pillows
in the long white sky.

II

Esperanto

1

The silky skin of the throat
where a kiss left a print, purple-brown
wings. How we kept going back to that place
with our mouths, my first
love and I. The beginners' course
in love and hurt. We wore our bruises
like a privilege, we wanted the world
to know we knew.

There was a life they would give us soon, it was
ours to be studied—the new word for *nipple, erect,*
irreversible, hook and *buckle,* for *when*
and *where*. Alert
as Jehovah's Witnesses,
one foot in the door.

The guide at the UN pointed up at the ceiling
of the great chamber: "The heating ducts are all
out in the open, look!"
No secrets, no war.
We admired the swanky staircase.
We put on headphones speaking
in seventy tongues.

2

A girl's got to think fast, in moves
of one syllable.
In my country, he said, the rooster
says *ku-ku-ri-ku,* the moon's
masculine.

25

I settled my head
on his shoulder ("Look wilted,
they like it"). You learn
to learn the idiom
when the heat's on.

Not chance! No such thing,
he winked. Somewhere
in another country, two people
just like us
are having this very same conversation.
He lifted his glass: *To us.*

3

I'm afraid to. Don't be. Slippery beads
on a string of silences, cool
and glassy to the touch. All the while stroking
my shoulder. And then
that humming like a ground bass, insistent,
beneath the syntax.

Unu du tri kvar kvin ses—
                                    Be sure to
master each lesson before you attempt
the next. *Domo:* house.
Fenestro: window. *Birdo:* a bird.

I wanted to say: "And after, what if I feel sad?"
but I kept forgetting the word for *after.*

                                4
All day I'd been waiting. He'd be back
any minute. Soon I'd
run down the hill, brush the grass from my skirt and

walk by, slow, with a practiced
indifference. *Hey, is that you?* I tried it out in the registers
of surprise. Too shrill. I sweetened it.
Grass stuck to my summer legs. I kept changing
hellos. If I picked up
the phone on the third ring, my lover

would leave his wife. We would have children,
new ones. I tucked them in, cranky, our own,
and turned out the light.

                                5
Some other lover taught me the code for
yes: two kisses on the eyelids, one long kiss
on the mouth. Every one of them
taught me. I studied
love. But now

I'm a married woman. You and I are a
man-and-wife, one flesh. *Married:*
you leave father and mother to become

that word. One word
for the hardness that needs to bury its head
in softness, the need that grows teeth,
the feast, the naked cleaving,
the flooding that can't stop itself
and the sadness, after.

6

I am scraping egg from the stacked dishes.
Married. Hot and cold water get married
in the faucet. Still married
and nothing I've ever learned will prepare me
for what I am learning.

You come into the kitchen, buttoning.
Seven buttons, belt-buckle, the chain-mail
watchband. Your mouth
blurs as it comes closer.

If I could bring you one clear word
that no one has ever—
                        I mean, even sex
is a silence
the body translates.

7

Under a baroque ceiling, the Serbs and Croatians
have begun to talk. *Peace, peace,* they say,
and it sounds like *piss.*
They won't smile, they won't look
at each other's faces, they won't
shake hands.

Once they shared a language. A hyphen
married them. *Have a Good Trip with*
ENA Motoring Oil the billboards piped
in Serbo-Croatian, down the coast road
of Yugoslavia. We were still
honeymoon-new:
one flesh, one language.

Now the UN translator is seated
in a baronial chair
between the two. Their angers
course through his body,
emerge as words.

8

Our chairs face each other across the room
even when we're gone.

9

Changing planes at midnight, not a syllable
left between us. You doze on a suitcase.
I'm alone, after. In a cramp
of envy, I watch
the Japanese man and Polish woman
find each other

in Esperanto. He's trying out
long and short smiles; she's got on
earnest crepe-soled shoes.
Hello! How are you! How good
to meet you!

They're going to save the world
with language. Pure language, boiled down
to the common solubles.
No national epics. No lovesongs. You can't
break your heart in a language
like that.

III

How the Last Act Begins

The trouble with you is you're not
loving enough. A drastic
summons, a trumpet of
hard last words.

I'm dry as a biscuit
but somehow a breast of mine
stiffens, unbuttons
and offers itself. Is that
what you want?

Now your body's in bed again, crying
that it can't fall asleep.
I forget what to feel, but I'll do
what I'm trained to do:
go barefoot, make the children
take off their shoes. You require
absolute silence.

The mind thinks "lemon" and the tongue
puckers. But what about the woman
who painted a tiger on the wall so real
it scared her out of the house?

I'm not making this up:
The three of us on tiptoe, the shades
down, the house darkened, and you
center-stage, wearing
that shiny black satin eye-mask.

Don't Tell the Children

1

Daddy's sad. Soon he'll be
happy again. A story I'm reading them
for the first time. Little spurts of
hot paint stain the page,
green spiky leaves.
They don't know the words yet.

I don't know the words.
I'm a child who has heard things
she shouldn't. Listening all night
at the grownups' door and I can't
make sense. Won't. I'm a child
hiding from my children.

2

Bedtime stories for the children: The cheetah is the fastest
land animal. It has tawny fur marked with black spots. It
is easily tamed. Giraffes are the tallest animals on earth.
They eat leaves from the tops of trees. Snails move very
slowly. They carry their shell-houses on their backs.

And for the grown-ups, an ancient tale: The war horse
says *Ha! ha!* among the trumpets. The eagle drinks blood.
The ostrich leaves her eggs in the dust. She forgets her
young. The bones of Behemoth are iron and brass.
Leviathan churns the waters to a boil. His nostrils are a
caldron; his breath, flame.

3

The children sit on the rumpled blankets
and listen. They listen hard.
They're getting it all down
for future reference. Tuned to our breath
they hear even the quarter tones.
They give off
vibrations too keen for the ear,
like a struck tuning fork that goes on trembling.

Crescendo

The children, squabbling
in the back bedroom: *You started. No, you
started first.* I can hear him too
with his right to be angry, his fists
pounding on their door.

When they pause for a moment
the noise of the world rises:
cars spattering the gutters, rain
driven hard against the glass.
The wind is searching out flaws in the plaster.

Last night the children couldn't sleep.
If anything happens to you, they asked
—and stopped, because
this is the life I've caulked and grouted,
where else would they go?

Then that pounding again: *Let me in!*
I pull the drapes shut.
The stubborn din in the skull
doesn't make a sound.

Crazed

We call glass *crazed* when it shatters like that.

The windshield of the car:
safety glass sculpted
by metal by fire by chance at eighty miles an hour
into swags of glittery spiderweb.

This time it was you, my love, my impossible,
who walked away from a death.
Where are you headed so fast,
so lost?

Shards of glass on the dented hood, in the powdery
dust of the junkyard.
A burst of crystals on the totalled front seat.
Light spikes from their sharpest edge
and sharpens it.

I take a handful home in my pocket for luck.

In my desk drawer they turn into teeth
cusped and hungry,
the hard inside of a mouth.

The Equilibrists

All year I've been trying to talk you
down from the ledge. Get down,
get down! I'll bring you hot milk and
rock you to sleep.

I'll put on my slingback heels, my red
lace nightie. Come, let me
unbutton your shirt, darling. What is it
you want?

Let's drive to Point Reyes, remember that
cabin out by the water,
there's an Italian movie you'll like
on Solano, how about a walk—

Think of the children! How can a father
of children
perch on a windowsill like a bird?

Here I am! you say, and lean forward
smiling, seductive:
What will you do now?

Compost

My hard carbuncular anger
scares me. This jackhammer rage.
Fever shakes me
till the whole house hurts. The heat
keeps building: peelings parings leaf-blades
blah blah of bright poison
bone meal and blood meal.

I want to stop him with one
annihilating word.
No, I won't say it. Let him
beg. Let him rise
on his hind legs and not get
the bone of an answer.

A soil of soils is breeding
in the smolder—a prize humus
to grow a marvel in,
some monstrous cabbage of a thousand leaves.
Oh my extravagant loam.
I shovel it under.

What It Takes

A dream of sugar on the stairs.
It pools underfoot
and I slip on it: every sweet
turns slippery. *Give me*

a little hug, you say, and lie down
on the sofa. Then you get up
and go back to bed.

On the dresser, a crumpled glove
like a lung
with the air gone out of it. On the bedspread,
a shaft of acid sun.

Don't you see I can't touch you? My hands
are snipped at the wrist
and sewn back with flimsy thread.
I have to hold them perfectly still.

We're the stunned
couple in the Hopper painting.
The woman stares out the window.
If this is what it's like, she thinks,
I can take it.

If this is what it takes, I will stay here
lying to myself, drowning
in shallow water.

Archipelago of Dreams

Those long-stemmed glasses, islands where I drift
in a viscous
sea of unsleeping, doped
on vodka and Benadryl,
the book dizzy in my hands.

Those glasses, crystal, a wedding gift
from my brother. We used to wash them by hand
and set them to dry on the striped towel.
I want to show you an amazing thing:
wine swirls and flames in a cracked glass
and the glass doesn't break

though fire, can you hear me? fire
is scorching the floorboards. *Help!*
Get help! And you
stand puzzled at the dream phone,
fumbling the yellow pages.

Then you're the hump of wet clay
on my back. *It's dead, shake it off.*
Who said that? I didn't know
that golem was you
till it lay in a pine box, eyes so pale
they were almost translucent.

Tonight we're at the coast again, swimming,
but we don't recognize each other.
The waves sting. Then the tide comes in,
our faces tilting the water
like dazed icebergs.

41

Puzzle Pieces

1

Sunlight in the alleys. There is always a window
to look out of. Barefoot,
in a half-slip, hair uncombed,
I stare at the buildings of red and brown brick,
the scaffolds abandoned for the weekend.

Before spring conceals them
the twig-ends of the trees are
knobby as grapestalks, fibrous, tensile.

And I never told you that—
was the way he started.
Then he looked away.

The seep of sunlight through the dusty blinds
is also a mooring.

2

I am threading silver filigree
through the squint of an earlobe.

Tickets, blue suitcase, phone number
scrawled on an envelope,
and through the window, two ladders
facing away from each other,
each casting a shadow on the sunlit wall.

If we'd gotten to the movies that night and if
his mother hadn't died and if the children
would only pipe down—

Stuck in the doorway, he waits,
a head on a stick of metal
on a block of stone.

Mother Hunger

1

Every knothole was a branch once.

The way her face dissolved
that time she went away: *I have to go, I have to*
his swollen *No, mama!* his wet
hands pulling
at her woolen skirt. He had to

stand there
stand there forever with the hired auntie and watch
as car after car of the long train
turned into steam.
Don't cry. You're a big boy now.

And then she was
back again, white-faced
mother of sorrows. A shriek at the window,
a worry on the shelf like a Meissen vase
a child mustn't break.

2

How the heat scatters her. A sudden whip
of wind. Here and there a bristly growth,
narrow leaves flinching.

They live in one close room,
a nest of flaking
newspapers. To have come
to this. Ten steps from bed
to dresser. Another five
to the door. And the child
clouding and polishing his face
in the family spoons.

Her child, after all. *You are my*
everything, she whispers,
and he nods.
Then that thirst rises in her—

                              She buries
her mouth in his cheek, his neck.

In the green bowl: heaped oranges,
the casual abundance of that other life.

3

Terrible always to be teetering
on stilts, those small wooden platforms
six inches off the ground.
He won't ever walk gracefully
though he's learning not to fall.

The applause that comes like a full stop
at the end of a sentence
is reward, or almost.
Still, he has to beg for it.

He wants to go down to the pond
after school like the others
and fish for tadpoles.
He'll take them home in a biscuit tin
with moss and water, a few twigs
to keep them company—
                          But there is papa
waving his arms again, shouting:
You must not worry mama.
And there is mama.

To live in their gaze
is to live in a house of glass.
Wherever he looks out
a severe love presses at the pane
looking in.

4

The child a palimpsest of his parents'
losses, each one slapped over
the last—wet paint of
swastikas on the windows
of that two-hundred-year-old house
and the money the maid stole
to help them get out and mama's
But if we get caught?—
red *J* of the passports, stamped
in the sweat of their hands.

Then that land of promises where the heat
flays the houses
where grass burns to khaki dust in the sun
where papa pedals uphill and
falls off the bike
dead at ten in the morning
just because it's over doesn't mean
it stops happening
and mama's still a little Ida in pigtails
crying in the corner.

He raises a puzzled face for her
pitying kiss. She's waiting for him.
It's her grief that flashes across
his old night sky. His hands shake
as hers did the year she died, he can't
hold a glass or write
his name on the line. Her terror
grips him. He turns
the soiled pages of his book
with her clumsy wet thumb.

Fooling the Enemy

His mouth twitches as he bends
to sign himself in.
I'm getting better, he says.
Do they know how sick I am?

Every morning he'd slap on a frantic cheer
like an old woman
with gummy rouge on her cheeks
to fool the enemy.

Now his camouflage has been stripped away.
He holds a hand to his face
to cover his nakedness.

I don't know that gray-haired child.
Don't know that woman either, that wife
who sits dumbly beside him, under
her dropcloth of calm.

She's the one in disguise now,
a lizard that stiffens and pretends
to be treebark. She won't move
even if you touch her
though panic
panic goes on pulsing her throat.

Straw Basket

She goes there every day on the way home from work.
At the corner of Milvia and Dwight
she slows down to take in the blinking Emergency sign,
the barred windows, like a bank's.

She has to ring the buzzer of Third Floor East to get in.
She recites her name to the metal ear of the door,
the small round strainer of names.
That's how she remembers who she is.

He'll be sitting on his bed with the shades down,
his eyes double-locked.
She says his name once, twice, but nothing opens.
Then a feeble smile passes over his face.
He offers her a fish-kiss, scaly, moist.

Today he holds out a straw basket
with a bunch of red wooden cherries on the lid.
Sullen and proud. *For you.* He won't look up.
He's just finished winding the wire stems around the handle.
And says, the way their sons used to say,
I made this for you.

Here

Anything
even the black
satin road where it catches
the streaked oils of stoplights
as I drive home alone
from the hospital
rain pocking the windshield
tires slicing the pooled water
to a spume taller than the car.
Even that patch where the road
fell in, rutted as a face, even that
cries out: Look at me
don't turn away, admit
the ravage is beautiful.
The world insists: I was here
before you and your pain,
I am here and I
will outlast you. *Yes,* says
the mind stroking itself
into life again
as a body, taking
what comfort
it can.

In the Ward

1

Soon nothing will be left but his *No*
that can't help itself,
can't stop, a phonograph needle
trailing a little clot of dust
that shudders when it touches down.

He sags on the bed till his face
falls into his hands.
Pitted gray pumice, moon-chalk
eroding into the acid air.

2

All year I dropped words into the well
of his silence. I could hear them
falling, could measure
the darkness they displaced.
I bent over the water and saw
my own face looking down.

Now he won't look at me.
He's watching the light
puddle on the floor: *I'm not listening.*

I hear a cave-sound
from inside him, a knucklebone scraping
an interior wall.

3

To the doctor he says,
They take care of you in the hospital.

And then slowly, after a pause, to himself,
I like
to be taken care of.

The doctor listens briskly, inspects
one shirt cuff, then the other, clean cotton
in a sheath of tweed.
Something starchy in him
crackles when he smiles.

4

Birds have eaten the breadcrumbs
and there is no moon.

Little hut in the forest,
how will I find you?

ECT

Whatever we forget is remembered somewhere.
—Yom Kippur liturgy

Electricity
scours his brain.
When they wheel him back
he has a just-wiped look on his face,
cool and shiny.
But where does the pain go?
The doctor wrings out the dishrag
and hangs it up to dry.

He can start over, revised,
an airbrushed photograph
with a girlish innocence around the eyes.
He's a tourist with only one shirt, and he's wearing it.
How light he feels.
He has dumped the cargo that made him founder,
the two-ton crates where rage
pounded in the nails.

"What's your name? Who's your wife?
Your children?"
His eyes flicker.
His new face, blank as an eggshell,
bobbles in the current.

Visiting Hours Are Over

Down the hall past the half-
closed doors
a body
crumpled on every bed
striped pajamas three pills
in a pleated cup past the windows
double-glazed against
the cold past the waxy
sansevieria past the lead apron
of hospital drapes
down the front steps into rain
two blocks to the car
I run
just to feel
my feet
slap the
pavement my hands
slam against my sides
cold wet
cold slippery wet
I don't
open the umbrella

IV

The Collector

1

The Roxie is down the street from the locked ward
where I left my husband.
I took the children to the movies that night,
a comedy about the war:
in the candy dark, the laughs
went off like explosions. Here's the letter he left me,
a green crayon scrawl. These
are the sayings I tacked to the wall
and the meager patience
I lace myself into. Here's the Primo Levi I carry
in my pocket: only catastrophe
will calm me. And here's
the comfortable voice of my so-called friend:
You had it too good.

2

I collect what he does
the way other people save string.
Bottle-tops, trivets, bone buttons
with tag-ends of thread in them, gritty
loose change—
                    I don't know how to sort or let go
so I stash it all, rusted feelings
without handles or wheels.

And the brain with its gullet, its coiled gut,
its gripping, its kneading, its
squeezing-of-the-damp-out
all day and all night—

57

3

The *shlup-shlup* of his slippers
down the hall to the kitchen
where he rules by gag law: *Don't say that.*
I'm a sick man. It's not my fault.

Yes. He's home again.
I shake the dry pod of my heart
and pray for a twitch of feeling,
a little rattle of love.

His fist pounding my shoulder
demands absolution.
I'm allowed two sentences: *You're fine.*
You're going to be fine.

Waking at Four

She didn't make this world,
this wincing sky. Didn't marry

the hands that grope for her
under the bedclothes

when the Halcion wears off.
Skullface, homunculus,

eyes locked in ice.
The forehead bulges, the jaws

slip away like soap, the legs
dwindle to a windsock.

He's in her bed.
I still love you, he says,

and his love clamps a hand
to the back of

her neck: I am yours,
I won't go away.

The Rule of Grammar

The past tense is so severe,
it makes everything
smaller.

I love you, we said
to each other
like that moment in running when both feet
are off the ground.

Clear and Cold

The leaves are brown paper bags.
What holds them to the tree
is a bit of twine.
I hate to say it, but I want them to fall.
I wanted my father to die when I knew
the doctors couldn't save him.
And I loved him.

I dreamed you were dead.
And I loved you. All that fury
of bloom when we started
unbuttoning, unzippering
singing *love, love,* to each other
sap rising in the trunk and streaming
streaming in the branches.

Now we're sad twins
dressed in the same starched pinafores.
We sit all day on the porch and stay clean.
And I loved you. Loved you.
I sat at my father's bedside
and watched him go.

The End of Safety

1

The children have vanished
into the free fall
of sleep. Now the house is quiet
though it makes little settling noises
like a cat licking itself
into calm. I lock the front door
and turn off all the lamps but one,
my gooseneck
with its sober island of light.

I have a pencil, a yellow pad, a glass of water,
and a ring on the fourth finger of my left hand
that my right hand keeps
turning and turning.

2

How I loved the calm of self-stick triangular corners.
The soothing black pages. The ceremony of choosing
what to save. How safe I felt
those long winter afternoons when rain
lulled the roof
as I sorted and cropped—

You, woman, you with both faces to the past,
enough! Why keep insisting it was wrong,
all wrong,
from the beginning? You, with your

interest in history, look at the two of us
feeding each other popcorn in living color
like all true lovers. Or kissing
in the kitchen, the crazy apron
tied around us both. In this one, can't you see?
I hold up the baby as proof
in the flickering shadow of the live oak.

                        3

Safety: a strip of amber
hall-light, insulation
under the door.

To live without looking, to be able
to lay your hand on
any cup on the shelf—

                        4

Do you love him? Yes, I still love him. *Do you
love him?* No.

Pain is carving me out so different
I can't go back. Not even if I want to

and I don't anymore.
What I have now

is who I am,
down to the bare worked wood.

And yet, says my hand-in-the-cupboard self. And yet.

5

Winter morning picks out the bare
branches of the fig tree: a thin-lipped
unblinking light.
I sit in the ladder chair without moving.

A smudge like an oily thumbprint
where a bird bruised the glass.
Where was it flying so possessed with air and light
before it fell?

Though You Haven't Asked

Because stones grow in the belly
like fists of salt—

Because the screen door keeps scraping,
swollen,
and won't stay closed—

Because the scar in the treebark
is larger every year—

Because you sit in the corner
and sulk—

I work the ring off and rub
my naked finger.

The ring's in my pocket.

Something is rolling downhill fast
gathering speed.

Before

This is the moment before the petals
drift to the tabletop.
The roses are open now, drooping

from their own spent weight.
He has backed into a corner, one hand
caught in a pocket, one hand across his chest

as if to defend himself. He brought her
the roses out of habit
or helplessness, which he calls

love: blown roses on impossible
spindle stems. Her eyes waver
as she turns away.

She hasn't told him yet
and he waits head down, though
he knows already.

Each time they speak, the words
open a little more heavily
on their stems.

A High Wind

rages in the house tearing sheets
from the mirrors slipcovers
from the chairs stripping
everything naked.
Lightning flares at the windows
zinc-white. All the sluices open.

A rack of branches on the sidewalk
like broken antlers. Only joy
with its floods
and fires
could be so cleansing.

I want to be out in this wind that can drive
a nail through a tree trunk. Let the
dead wood fall!
There is still time to say what the two of us
never dared—

Let it bring the house down.

The Kiss

There was a ghost at our wedding,
the caterer's son,
who drowned that day.

Like every bride I was dressed
in hope so sharp
it tore open
my tight-sewn fear.

You kissed me under the wedding canopy,
a kiss that lasted a few beats longer
than the usual,
and we all laughed.

We were promising: the future
would be like the present,
even better, maybe.
Then your heel came down
on the glass.

We poured champagne
and opened the doors to the garden
and danced
a little drunk, all of us,

as the caterer made the first cut,
one firm stroke, then
dipped his knifeblade
in the water.